A Book for You

A Book for You

An anthology in tribute to
Shaykh Muhammad Hisham Kabbani
28 January 2016

© Copyright 2016 Institute for Spiritual and Cultural Advancement. All rights reserved.

Printed and bound in the United States of America. No part of this book may be reproduced in any form or by any electronic or mechanical means, including information storage and retrieval systems, without permission in writing from the publisher, except by a reviewer, who may quote brief passages in a review.

Published and Distributed by:

Institute for Spiritual and Cultural Advancement (ISCA)
17195 Silver Parkway, #201
Fenton, MI 48430 USA
Tel: (888) 278-6624
Fax: (810) 815-0518
Email: staff@naqshbandi.org
Web: http://www.naqshbandi.org

First Edition: June 2016
A Book For You: An anthology in tribute to Shaykh Muhammad Hisham Kabbani/
ISBN: 978-1-938058-31-8

Library of Congress Cataloging-in-Publication Data

Kabbani, F Sajeda.
 A Book For You: An anthology in tribute to
Shaykh Muhammad Hisham Kabbani/ Sajeda F. Kabbani
 1 volume--ECIP data.
 Includes poetry
 ISBN 978-1-938058-31-8 (alk. paper)
 1. Sufism I. Title.
 KBP144.K33 2014
 340.5'9--dc23
                              2014019237

PRINTED IN THE UNITED STATES OF AMERICA
15 14 13 12 11 05 06 07 08 09

Table of Contents

Dedication..1
Introduction 3
Narratives..5
Poems 97
Illustrations 121

بسم الله الرحمن الرحيم

Dedication

May Allah Almighty send peace and blessing upon Sayyidna Muhammad ﷺ and on the Family of Sayyidna Muhammad. Our Guide has taught us of the great poets who wrote about the Prophet ﷺ. Through his teachings, he emphasized the tremendous importance of expressing our love to the Prophet ﷺ, as those poets did. With this intention, this book was born to illustrate the love we have for our Guide, Shaykh Hisham Kabbani, for surely he is the representation of the Holy Prophet, Sayyidna Muhammad ﷺ, in our time. May Allah Almighty bless him and keep us to be with him in this life and the next insha'Allah.

Introduction

To the one who is the best of those in this day and age. To the one who is the light that takes all heartache away, and to the one who is the most beloved to me. This book is for you. The words that fill these pages are nothing but expressions of love for you. You've touched so many people with just your smile. A smile that is engraved into my mind's eye. A smile that without I wouldn't know how to carry on.

You've been there for all of us. For me from my first memory. You've been there all these years, teaching me, carrying me, and loving me and that's more than I deserve. I pray Allah Almighty gives you the longest and healthiest of lives because more than we need air or more than we need the sweet taste of water, we need you, for surely you are the representation of the Prophet ﷺ.

Having you in my life is worth more than this whole world and everything that inhabits it. Without you, I would be lost—we all would. When I think about the next life, all I can see is your face. As the Holy Messenger ﷺ said, "You will be resurrected with the ones you love," and nothing makes my heart more at ease, for even though I don't know whether or not I will be permitted into Jannah, I do know that I love you with a love that is true and that loving you will save me. And I know that even when Allah Almighty has called you to His Divine Presence, I will be reunited with you because of this hadith you taught us—a hadith more valuable to me than anything because it ensures that I and all of us who love you will be with you in this life and the next insha'Allah.

You are the greatest gift Allah Almighty has bestowed upon this Earth. If only everyone knew how lucky they are to have even passed you by in the street. I don't know what we did to have the honor of seeing you every day, to sit with you, to learn from you, to see your smile. Sometimes we forget how especially lucky we are, and this is a great offense to you and to The One who gave you to us. Forgive us, forgive me, if even for a second we haven't showed you the love or respect that you deserve or if for a moment we took you for granted.

Your love and support has always been there for me, for all of us, and I hope to do even a fraction for you as you have done for me. If my actions fail, know that my love for you never will. Truly you are the best of those in this day and age. Truly you are the one who takes all heartache away and truly, truly you are the most beloved to me.

Narratives

I have had the great blessing of spending many years as a student of Mawlana Shaykh Hisham, and he has taught me innumerable things. One of the biggest things that he has taught me and many others is the importance of the respect for the Prophet Muhammad ﷺ and for his Family and Companions. An example of this is he taught us about Mawlid an-Nabi, the celebration of the birth of the Prophet ﷺ, and about struggle.

I am an American Muslim who had never heard of Mawlid before I met Mawlana Shaykh Hisham in 1994. First, he realized that most American Muslims (like myself) and most masajid in America either didn't know about or didn't accept the celebration of Mawlid. So he worked to change that.

First, he printed books on the permissibility of celebrating Mawlid from a scholarly perspective. He distributed these pamphlets at Islamic conferences, and they tried to make him leave. Then he started spreading the good word of the Mawlid – from discussions with students and hosting Mawlid celebrations. Then he printed books on Mawlid with an English transliteration and translation. His beautiful wife, Hajjah Naziha, would lead ladies Mawlid. Then his beautiful daughter, Sajeda, and his beautiful granddaughter, Naziha, formed a singing group with other young ladies that sing beautiful Mawlid songs.

And at every one of these points there were tremendous obstacles that rose up to try and stop him. And he persevered in teaching the love and respect for Sayyidna Muhammad ﷺ. Now, through the support of Allah Azza wa Jal, and with Mawlana Shaykh Hisham's hard work and perseverance, the Mawlid is widely celebrated everywhere around America and in England. Mawlana Shaykh Hisham's hard work and abilities and their result are a *burhan*, proof, he is a reviver of the religion. It is a proof that he is the best living example of the Prophet Muhammad (s).

We are so grateful to him for his strength and bravery and pray always for him and his family to have the longest of lives and best of health.

My Beloved Shaykh, whom I have witnessed save hundreds of thousands of souls, to teach them to love their Lord, to obey and love His Divine Messengers and to 'obey those in authority over you.' Most of all, you guide us to the Threshold of the Sultan of All Saints, Our Most Beloved and Revered Master, Sayyidina Muhammad (salAllahu alayhi wa sallim). For this act alone, if all the oceans where ink and the trees were pens, I could not sing the praises that are due to my Beloved Shaykh Hisham Al-Kabbani, who has tolerated my bad manners and excused my ignorance and continued to raise me into Manhood. To serve God Almighty is to serve His Creation.

Thank you for opening your home to us, for being an inspirational leader, guide, and teacher. Your compassion and character are inspiring and beautiful, and Insha'Allah we can follow your example. It means the world to me to have someone to whom I can bring any question; to have a role model. There are so many Muslims around the world who have no direction, but Alhamdulillah you provide a direction for me and countless others. Your entire family has opened their homes and hearts to everyone who is in need of help, and I am forever grateful to all of you.

You and your family deserve the very best for all that you have done for the Muslim Ummah. I wish all of you long, happy, healthy lives, and hope to continue learning from you and Hajjah Naziha.

A man became my greatest gift from a divine treasury. He teaches us how to seek Gods face through a Muhammadan reality. He is Father, Mother, Pilot, Sage, the keys to all my prayers. He is a love that transcends time and space—a man truly aware. It has been said once before his true beauty we've not beheld, but my prayer is that during our lifetime from his love we are not veiled.

Thank you Mawlana for showing me the beauty and love of Islam. Without your influence and guidance, I know for sure I would be lost in the darkness of this dunya. You are my light, my guide. Any big problem in my life has been fixed thanks to your prayers, your advice always taking me in the right direction. You foster the love of Allah Almighty and the Prophet ﷺ in my heart. I could never repay you for all you've done for me. May Allah bless you and grant you a long healthy life.

Throughout my life, Mawlana Shaykh Hisham has saved me both directly and indirectly from countless hardships. He is important to me because he is my guardian in this life and in the next life Insha'Allah. Mawlana Shaykh has never interacted with me in any manner other than love, even when I deserved the opposite. That overwhelming unconditional love is something that I hold very dear. He is my teacher, my sultan, and my closet ally when I need him. Because of his love and leadership, I've been able to climb the most challenging hurdles that life has given me and for that I am forever grateful. He is our rock; without him we are nothing.

Dearest Mawlana Shaykh Hisham,

My name is Soraya, and I am 10 years old. I will never forget the day my family and I met you for the first time. It was in Marrakech, in April 2015. My paternal grandparents, my parents, my uncle and I, had made the trip from Tangiers, only in the hope of meeting you.

My father was able to obtain the name of the residence where you were staying at. Not knowing whether we would find you there, we thought we would leave a few gifts from Morocco for you and your family. Following a man's invitation at the entrance of the residence, my mother went in first and walking towards the patio, she met you, you and your noble wife, as you were coming down the stairs. As soon as she saw you, my mother was full of emotions, and you greeted her warmly. You invited all of us to sit on the patio, and we remained in your noble presence discussing for over half an hour. You also had to go to an appointment, but you spontaneously postponed it to welcome us and host us.

As my mother was pregnant, at the end of our meeting, I asked you if you could give a name for the baby, which you did kindly. Six months later, my mother gave birth to my little brother, and thus we called him Adam Nour El Haq.

This sweet moment spent with you will remain forever engraved in my memory. It was the best meeting since my parents took me to Lefke to visit Mawlana Shaykh Nazim (qaddas Allahu sirruhu) in 2011. I hope to meet you again one day. Happy Birthday Mawlana! I love you from the bottom of my heart!

Love,
Soraya from Morocco (with my daddy's help)

Happy Birthday, Mawlana! You have given me everything beautiful and good in my life. Gazing on your countenance, so like the full moon in its light and beauty, was enough of a favor for a lifetime. Still you have given my family and I so much more.

You have taken us on Hajj and allowed us to travel with you. We have seen hundreds of thousands of people yearning for you, attending your Mawlid. Seen you as a Beacon of Light and Guidance for them and us. You have shared your blessed family with us. We are so unbelievably blessed to have been in that light, to be in that light. You took me to see Mawlana Shaykh Nazim. In your generosity and graciousness, you introduced me as "generous." Then Mawlana Shaykh Nazim spoke the truth. He said, "Shaykh Hisham, you are the most generous one." You are truly the epitome of generosity. I am only with you because of your generosity because Allah Almighty knows I do not deserve it. I have disobeyed you too much.

Please forgive me. Keep us in your heart and your gaze always on us. May Allah lengthen your life and grant you endless happiness with your children and Hajjah Naziha. May He lengthen your life with my life because a world without you is not a world worth living in.

There I was sitting with Shaykh Hisham and another man, the three of us alone and talking about what's going on in the world. At this time in life I had been struggling with ridding myself of bad habits to be clean, like the shaykh recommends. However, I never brought this up to Shaykh Hisham physically, nor would I ever mention it in the company of others. As we sat together, I noticed Shaykh Hisham began to change the topic to a story about Grandshaykh AbdAllah encouraging someone to quit smoking and I began to panic inside because I was scared my shaykh was going to call me out. However, once the topic started to shift I noticed all of his attention shifted as well, but surprisingly not to me, his eyes were entirely focused on the man sitting with us, who I know did not struggle with that issue.

He continued with the story and described for us the willpower it takes for humans to leave our bad habits and bad characters behind us, all the while never looking at me. Then it dawned on me as his story ended, he never looked at me but that story was entirely meant for me; in his subtle, gracious way he taught me a lesson and supported me without humiliating me. I would have been shy to speak to him alone and I would have been mortified if I was corrected in front of others. He knew exactly how to guide me and correct me in a way I could bear. That is the profound wisdom of a true master, not only knowing the issue without being told but to also administer the perfect solution.

This is just one simple experience with Shaykh Hisham Kabbani that stuck with me because it gave me an idea of what it means to have perfected manners.

We love you, Shaykh Hisham.

Mawlana Shaykh Hisham, is like a never ending ocean of love. He can take you out of the greatest depths of darkness and fill every corner of it with light. I can't imagine what my life would be like if it wasn't for my beloved teacher Shaykh Hisham. Any moment of sadness disappears just by remembering him. Every difficulty I have faced, by his baraka and du`as, becomes easy and small. There is no one alive today like him, who has touched more hearts and saved more people. The positive impact he has on everyone, even those who have only seen him once, is phenomenal. Many of my non-Muslim friends are always astonished when they see him and even years later hold him in high respect.

We were told to share experiences and miracles but the fact is Shaykh Hisham is a miracle. Nowhere else have I ever seen so many people, with so many different backgrounds, races, colors, etc., come together as one with love to one another. This is due to the teachings of Shaykh Hisham and the bridges he has built and his emphasis on unity. In these days of confusions, Sayyidi is the opener of truth and the one who has revived the Love of Prophet ﷺ across the globe.

"You will be resurrected with those whom you love" I love Shaykh Hisham. Insha'Allah May Allah (Almighty) grant him a longer, healthy, happy, blessed life and the same for his family. Insha'Allah may we celebrate his birthday in the time of Sayyidna Mahdi (as) and Sayyidna Isa (as) Happy birthday and we love you!

At the most difficult moments in my life, Mawlana Shaykh Hisham Kabbani has been the only person on whom I could rely. I will be forever grateful that Allah Almighty made our paths to cross and honored me with such a rare guide. I have watched him closely over many years and seen his own dynamic growth. He has made me see the true value in giving my full effort. He is the best example of what true submission looks like. In fact, he has made me believe that even the loftiest goals are indeed attainable. In short, he has believed in me when no one else did-especially not me.

There was a time in my life where I was unable to sleep at all for nearly two months. Even with the aid of sleeping pills, I could only sleep two hours. However, the sleeping pills were making me terribly forgetful. I tried to sleep by making salawat one night. I made salawat for six hours and was unable to sleep. The next day, Mawlana looked at me and said lie on your right side and make salawat-you will fall asleep right away. I went to bed that night, on my right side while making salawat. I slept in two minutes. I have been able to sleep like this for years now. That is one of the many times in my life that Allah has granted something beautiful to me through the hands of our wonderful Shaykh. May Allah Almighty bless him and shower him in endless mercy and favors in dunya and Akhirah.

Life has never been the same after meeting Mawlana for the first time. Being raised in a Muslim family and living in a Muslim country was a blessing, but oh how little I knew of my deen until I was exposed to a night of dhikrullah held at the University of British Columbia where I met Mawlana and Hajjah for the first time.

It was a night never to be forgotten, as I sat there with my three young girls, the majestic power of recitation and the presence of Mawlana was so powerful for my littleness, a stream of tears accompanied me for the rest of the evening. That was the night I entered Islam with its beauty and love!

I thank Allah Almighty for all His immense blessings, the most important being, the guidance in understanding deen, and life through a very kind and loving teacher Mawlana Shaykh Hisham Kabbani. His humble kind nature is a constant source of inspiration for me to be on a path of self-improvement.

May Allah Almighty bless our beloved Mawlana with immense nobility and infinite, loving mercy.

It is hard to put into words how I feel about Mawlana. I can't even begin to understand everything that he does for all of us, and the burdens that he carries for us every day. In addition to everything he protects us from, he brings a great deal of love and light to our lives. There is one example of this that I will never forget.

I had been married for about five years, and my husband and I had wanted children right away, but no baby came. I was beginning to fear that it would never happen. One day, we had the opportunity to invite Mawlana for dinner. I remember talking to him on the phone, and saying that it might be better if we ate at my parents' house, as they had more space. At the time we didn't even have a dining table. Mawlana said, "No." He said he wanted to come to our house and that he could sit on the floor. Though I was ashamed not to be able to offer more to him, of course we agreed, and he came and ate dinner at our house. Later that night at the mosque, he mentioned the dinner, and before he left he prayed over me. He said that I would have a baby soon. To my amazement and great joy, I found out about a month later that I was expecting my eldest son.

This is just one example of the many miracles that happen because of Mawlana. May Allah grant him a long, blessed life, and immense happiness. And may Allah forgive me for not being more grateful every day that I have him in my life.

THE CIRCLE FORMULA

$(X-H)^2 + (Y-K)^2 = r^2$ (H,K) are the x,y coordinates of the center of the circle. We can see the deeper meaning of HK (Shaykh Hisham's initials) as wherever he travels, he represents the center of our circles of dhikr, always guiding us in the ways of Mawlana Shaykh Nazim and the Naqshbandi Golden Chain.

Teaching us to spend time and prayer and giving alms,
No one's words are more beautiful than Shaykh Hisham's,
The radius points to the center of the circle (H,K),
If we follow him and footsteps of saints, we will be okay,
Taking from holy notes of the Masters of the Golden Chain,
For sure, upon his listeners showers of Mercy will rain,
Prayers for all of us is what we ask him to say,
And insha'Allah, we find our lives blessed and happy every day.

Wishing you many blessings and happiness, Mawlana!

Shaykh Hisham Kabbani, what can I say about the one who Allah has placed his image in the Orion Nebula? We existed from pre-eternity. The white light I see in you is the same as in me. We are all made of the same light. Your light is of the sword of La ilaha illa-Llah, cutting through darkness and disbelief.

You are the most excellent of guides, the Sultan of the Heavens and the Master of the self. You have taught me everything I know about Islam and Tariqah through guidance and your enlightened suhbahs. We are in safe hands with you, leading us to the endless delight of the oceans of the Beloved of Allah.

It was one of those cold winter nights, just like this one, when I first arrived in this country. I came here to start a new life, far away from the place I had called home for many years. It seemed quite impossible at that time that I would be able to feel at home here one day, but you, ya Sayyidi, have always welcomed me warmheartedly. It was one of those cold winter nights, just like this one, when I came to realize that home isn't a place, it is a person. May Allah Subhanahu wa Ta'ala give you a long life, health and happiness and allow us to be in your blessed company always. Ameen.

One glance at their beautiful face and I found inner peace—the way they spoke, how they carried themselves with such a divine grace. Some speak ill of them, but I pay no heed, for how can one even deny such a good deed? They are raised amongst the Awliya, like the earth and the horizon, and we are nothing but dirt in comparison. So humble in their speech that is beyond one's reach, so how do I describe to be worthy of their mureed? Now some say this thought is flawed, and this idea should be withdrawn, but I say there is never a beautiful rose without a thorn. We are nothing but mere dust, but we hold tight on a rope which is called trust. Through my Shaykh I found Allah, and only through Allah I found my Shaykh! For surely Allah is The Best of Planners! We love you Mawlana Shaykh Hisham.

I have so many memories of Mawlana, it is hard to choose. He is truly amazing and there are no words to describe him. He always made me feel welcome, and I always felt so shy at how humble and caring he is for others. There was a time when he and Hajjah sat me down and said since both my sisters were planning on getting married and having a big wedding, they wanted me to have a wedding also. Since I had the great blessing to be married by Mawlana in his house two years ago, I did not want to have a large wedding when they had done so much for me already, I didn't want to trouble them with marrying us again. They insisted though and paid for my wedding dress. Just writing this makes me cry, because they showed me such love and there are no words to say how much I love Mawlana and Hajjah.

Traveling and living with them at times in the same house was such a blessing, and I dream of being able to do that again one day. Insha'Allah they can forgive me for all the mistakes and bad adab I made and for any pain or trouble I caused them. Knowing them has brought me true happiness. If I did not have them in my life, I do not know where I would be right now.

Happy Birthday, Mawlana. May Allah Almighty bless you and give you more and more strength and support with a long and healthy life. May we be with you dunya and Akhirah.

All of us in my family are wishing that Allah Almighty grants you a very long life and good health. On the blessed occasion of your birthday, I'm reminded of what a great blessing it is to have you in our lives. We pray for you and your family every day. We love you all. I ask Allah Almighty that, despite my multitude of faults, we are included in your company and that of our blessed Sultan Mawlana Shaykh Nazim in the Hereafter and insha'Allah with the Most Beloved Messenger of Allah, Sayyidina Muhammad ﷺ.

Alhamdulillah meeting Shaykh Hisham Kabbani happened within two weeks after I begged Allah Subhanahu wa Ta'ala to bring me to an authentic shaykh. I longed for genuine spiritual communion and was disheartened by so many imposters. The next day I received email, an invitation to hear Mawlana speak at an event, my long anticipated, Heaven-sent opening!

I always kept my experience with Mawlana Shaykh Hisham very private, but when I heard about the fitna people were making on him, I wrote my story on Facebook.com/MiraclesInIslam. I wanted to share my experience and love for him. I can say with all of my heart and not an atom of doubt in my mind, that Mawlana Shaykh Hisham is a Miracle of Islam. He demonstrates only the greatest goodness, the purest sweetness, the sincerest humility, and the most righteous actions, the most selfless generosity, and the highest morality of all people. For sure, he is the best man living on this Earth today. I know he is my shaykh and my guide and he is carrying everything in this universe, and we are so lucky to have his love and his hand over our heads. By the baraka of Rasulullah ﷺ and Grandshaykh AbdAllah and Sultan al-Awliya Mawlana Shaykh Nazim, may Mawlana Shaykh Hisham receive more heavenly support and power, the best of health, and the longest life.

My miracle with Mawlana Shaykh Hisham and Mawlana Shaykh Nazim isn't like the 'miracles' you imagine; it is simple, but it is a miracle to me. I was born into the Tariqah and my parents loved and obeyed Mawlana Shaykh Nazim and Mawlana Shaykh Hisham, who was appointed to guide those in the west. My parents took us to see Mawlana Shaykh Hisham when he came to New York/New Jersey because that was the closest place to our home he came, so we saw him once or twice a year through our childhood. We saw Mawlana Shaykh Nazim, may Allah bless his soul, two times when he came to New York and Washington DC. We grew up with love and respect for them and alhamdulillah we had their guidance and physical presence since we were children.

When I became a teenager and went into high school, I started to struggle a lot. We lived in a small town in America with no other Muslims at the school and no Muslim friends around to relate to, so we made non-Muslim friends and I fell into haram things, astaghfirullah. Anytime I was doing something haram, Mawlana Shaykh Hisham would immediately come to my mind, and I would feel very ashamed. But I still struggled, the western side and western values were pulling me and my parents were trying to pull me to Islamic ways and for 1 year it was like that. I happened to be the most popular girl at school with all the students and the teachers. As a top athlete and with the best grades, everyone admired and loved me and put me up on a pedestal. Obviously this gave me a sense of happiness and excitement, but I always knew it wasn't real love or success, it wasn't a path to Allah Almighty's love, but I continued to struggle and by the end of the school year, my mom was very worried and upset with me, and one day she yelled at me and asked "You don't listen to your mother! You don't listen to your father! Who will you listen to then? Who do you trust?" I answered, "Mawlana Shaykh Hisham." I believe that this trust in him came from the baraka of my parents' love for him and from them taking us to see him every year. We knew he was our guide and could feel him present in our lives and in our hearts, no matter how much we struggled.

Immediately, we got advice from him and he said it was good for me to come to live there, in Michigan. So, I went, with no hesitation, and a lot of people who didn't understand were upset, "why are you leaving? You have everything here." Many teachers and coaches called my mother to tell her I shouldn't go, even some family members didn't agree, but it didn't matter. We knew that he knew what was best for me. I knew that all of the many pleasures in my life felt like nothing compared to the pleasure of being near Mawlana Shaykh Hisham. He has something so special, which fills your heart with light and contentment that surpasses anything in this dunya.

At that time, I could really feel that the love I had from so many people was not important, all that mattered was working towards the love of our Shaykh and our Prophet ﷺ and Allah Almighty. So by the baraka of Mawlana Shaykh Hisham, I was able to see this very quickly and when I was sixteen, I moved away from home to live in Michigan. I finished high school there and within one year of living there, I was a completely different person. In the two years I lived there, I tasted the reality of Islam, the true Islam that our hearts long for, the tasteful way of life that our souls ache for. This Islam and this community exists there only because of Mawlana Shaykh Hisham.

Under the order of Sultan al-Awliya, Mawlana Shaykh Hisham came to the West. He brought Islam to a land of non-Muslims. It is a huge task that no one else could do as successfully as him. He brought the light of Islam and the love of Rasulullah ﷺ to the West and so many hearts were attracted, so many non-Muslims became Muslim, so many Muslims came to a better understanding of their religion and love of Rasulullah ﷺ.

Shaykh Hisham emanates light in a time and place full of darkness, he instills faith in those who otherwise would have never found it, he guides those who are lost, and he gives a love that no one has ever felt before.

It was only because of his love, that I was able to leave behind everything and everyone I knew in my life. It was only because of his generosity and kindness and love, that I found peace in this life and within myself. It is only because of his power and continuous support, that we are practicing our Islam and trying to be good in a time where it is so difficult to do so.

Having him in America has been an immeasurable blessing. It is as if we always had Mawlana Shaykh Nazim with us in our country through the years because we had Shaykh Hisham, his greatest lover. And he takes care of us, and knows our hearts inside and out, and has the heavenly power to guide us. He saved us and continues to save us every day. He welcomes us in his home, despite our many shortcomings and dirty egos. This is something else that amazes me. If you look at all the kings and queens, presidents and diplomats, scholars and people in power, they would never invite common people to eat with them and visit with them. It would be completely absurd for them and the amazing thing is, Mawlana Shaykh Hisham is in a higher position than all of them, but look how he invites even the least important people into his home, it doesn't matter if you are wealthy or poor, high status or no status, Muslim or non-Muslim, mindful or mindless, he sits with everyone. This is true humility and generosity. He feeds so many people and sits with anyone who wants to come and treats everyone with so much respect despite his most high knowledge and position. Masha'Allah! Words cannot explain.

Prophet ﷺ said, "No one humbles himself for the sake of Allah, but Allah will raise his status." Then for sure Allah Almighty has raised Mawlana Shaykh Hisham in a way we cannot comprehend.

How can I describe you? How can I express my love to you? When every moment with you is precious and special, how can I choose? I see you much more than others, and yet sometimes I feel like I'm not seeing you at all. When you're angry, I feel it. When you're sad I want to cry. How do I help you? How can I help you? How do I show my love for you? I can't write poems. I can't write emotional, inspiring stories. I can't write songs for you. But I love you. I just don't know how to show my love for you.

It is impossible to praise you with words as your mentioning is beyond what words can merely describe. You are an embodiment of the Sunnah, the King of all people.

I cannot imagine where I would be without you, Mawlana. You are the reason I maintain a smile in a situation of darkness, as the thought of you comes into my heart. As I know your love for us is greater than how much we could ever love you, and you wish for us more than that which you wish for yourself, and that one glimpse of the most beautiful face I have seen will suffice for me to always stay happy.

When love comes to my mind I think of no one but you, for you have saved me alongside millions of others from misguidance. A day cannot go by without your remembrance; my only wish is to be with you for eternity Insha'Allah.

A million words will not give justice to whom you really are and how much I love you. Forgive us for our shortcomings and please always hold onto our hands. May Allah Almighty give you happiness for eternity, and give you a long and happy life alongside your blessed family, and may He Almighty continue to raise your great station and sanctify your secret.

We love Mawlana very much, and are so grateful for everything he has done for us. We wish you a most happy and blessed birthday and hope you have a long and happy life. Thank you for everything!

I pray my Lord, You may grant Your blessings always eternally upon Muhammad ﷺ, his Companions and his Family. I wish you, Mawlana, many, many happy returns on this beautiful day.

I cannot appreciate the beauty you brought into my life. Before you, there was nothing, and with you there is everything. Life became beautiful when I was blessed with your presence. There was darkness in the four corners of the room and now I see nothing but light. I am so lucky that the Lord Almighty blessed me and my family with a righteous leader as yourself.

Love is very hard to find in this modern day and age. Therefore, I was so fortuitous to find you and be able to pray for your long life. You are all I pray for, and I just wish that you continue to warm the hearts of all your mureeds as you have mine. Out of the darkness you are the shining star that guides me towards my destination. You have brought me towards Islam, to the righteous path and, most importantly, the Lord Himself. You have become my beautiful sunrise after a dark night.

I love you up to the Highest Heaven and back. Whenever I see you, you make me smile. I've had many experiences with you and every one of them was great. Even when you're traveling, I know that you will always be in my heart, and be with me by spirit. I don't think that anyone has ever been disappointed with your choices, and I don't think anyone is sad when they're around you. May Allah give you a long and healthy and happy life. Ameen!

11.04.15: the day I felt alive again. The day where you were throwing blessed sweets at the northerners, and I was praying you would throw one at me. Little did I know the sweet I was about to be given. Something beautiful Shaykh Shair said to me was, "You have nothing to worry about, since the day Mawlana took you upstairs he's been protecting you. Do your bit." Alhamdulillah wa shukrulillah for such a guide. In your form, we see our Beloved Mawlana Shaykh Nazim. Happy birthday, Mawlana. May Allah grant you many more happy years and may you continue to visit us every year with good health! We love you, we love you, we love you so much! We love you what else can we say? Shaykh Hisham!

Oh Shaykh Hisham, I always yearn to be in your presence, but I never get the chance. I always make intention to go to your events, but I never get the chance. I used to think that my connection with Mawlana Shaykh Nazim was gone, but that night you came in my dream and said "Never think your connection is gone, it will always be there, do not worry." Ever since then, it gave me relief and satisfaction.

When I see your beautiful face it gives me peace in my heart. You remind me of our Beloved Prophet ﷺ. Mawlana Shaykh Nazim may have physically departed from us, but his spirit still lives in you, his teaching still lives in you, his love still lives in you, everything about him still lives in you and forever it will. I see him in you Ya Shaykh Hisham and forever I will. I love you Shaykh Hisham and forever I will. I will forever wait until the day we meet. "Oh how sweet is eternity, eternity, eternity," as Mawlana Shaykh Nazim said. Happy Birthday, ya Sayyidi, I pray you have a very long life Insha'Allah!

Mawlana Shaykh Hisham is one of the servants of Allah Almighty who makes the love of Rasulullah ﷺ boil in the hearts of people. He makes people understand the essence of iman and the Oneness of Allah Almighty. He preserves the path of love and peace and guides people on the same path. He explains in the most lucid way the nitty-gritty of Islam. He guides people to Allah Almighty through Rasulullah ﷺ. For him the spirit of Rasulullah ﷺ is paramount to attain the love of Allah Almighty.

He is linked to the Golden Chain of Naqshbandi Shaykhs that have a bond with Rasulullah ﷺ through Hazrat Abu Bakar Siddiq ؓ. He is the most trustworthy hand-hold that never breaks. As reported in Qur'an:

Let there be no compulsion in religion: Truth stands out clear from Error. Whoever rejects evil and believes in Allah hath grasped the Most Trustworthy hand-hold that never breaks and Allah heareth and knoweth all things. (Surat al-Baqara, 2:256)

Mawlana Shaykh Hisham is attached to Rasulullah ﷺ and he, in turn, attaches people to Rasulullah ﷺ. There is every hope that people who follow Mawlana Shaykh Hisham will one day see the beautiful radiant face of Rasulullah ﷺ and will land in Allah Almighty's Love and Mercy.

While I found the notion of joining a mystical Sufi order appealing, the prospect of having to actually follow the practices of one of the world's more demanding religions did give pause. So, I suppose that's where our shaykh's come in – they can bridge things for us when big steps are required. Shaykh Hisham can be both disarming and direct, and so, as I worked through a reception line after a dhikr one evening in the mid-nineties, Shaykh Hisham grabbed my arm and launched into Shahadah.

Well, as John Lennon said, "Life is something that happens to you while you're making other plans." That particular evening was a turning point in my life and that of my family, as well. Sometimes you connect the dots in your life only after the facts. I did later remember that as a child I had a recurring vision of three men in robes and turbans motioning with their arms to come and join them. No words were spoken – their faces I can no longer remember. It was more a feeling of being asked to join something. And there was Shaykh Hisham that night, all those years later, not only welcoming me, but holding onto my wrist, saying words I only vaguely understood, but it all seemed right somehow: an invitation and a decision made easy.

Well, it's been an interesting twenty years: good years, I might add. It is said that each shaykh carries a particular set of attributes all his own. My guess is that our teacher, Shaykh Hisham, can see into us clearly enough to grab us at the right moment and confidently aim us in a new direction, smiling as he does so, with one eye on us, and the other on Shaykh Nazim quietly nodding in approval as he looks on from that magical place where all visions and blessings must originate.

Like every murid, I remember the first time I met Mawlana Shaykh Hisham like it was yesterday. It was Spring 1996, before his legendary 1st International Islamic Unity Conference in Los Angeles when he travelled to many mosques and groups to speak on Tariqah and sometimes even to fundraise for them. This gathering was a mix of practicing and non-practicing Muslims, others who were curious about Tariqah, some who needed advice or du`a, Americans, foreigners, people who spoke different languages, and a few murids.

One man asked, "What is the role of a shaykh?" Mawlana replied, "A shaykh is really a doctor who sees your ailments and pokes them so the sickness comes out and he can replace it with Light and heal you."

How profound. Somehow I knew everything he said was customized to touch the heart of every person there and that blew my mind.

May Allah Almighty continue to raise him and bless him and his family. We thank you, and we love you and ask for your forgiveness. No words can touch on your realities.

I was searching for a path, studied about different paths, and finally found my beloved Shaykh's wisdom. Still I am not a mureed and am waiting for the day to hold his hand insha'Allah. I saw a dream that our beloved Mawlana was at the door to a room permitting visitors to enter to the room. I also heard that our Master Muhammad ﷺ was in this room. Our Mawlana gave me a pass to enter the room. It was unexplainable—Allah Kareem.

I sincerely wish you to be in excellent health and enduring long-life to continue your good works in giving much-needed advice and inspired guidance to all the mureeds everywhere around the world.

I once dreamt of you, Mawlana Shaykh Hisham, appearing to me with your very bright Nur resembling the Sun, and in another I had of you, you came and acknowledged an old faded Indonesian batik jacket which I had put on. Dear Shaykh Hisham, please forgive me, for I am a very weak soul. I humbly apologize to you from the bottom of my heart for anything I've done to let you down.

Happy Birthday to My Beloved Murshid, may Allah give you a long life to guide us in this time of many troubles. O Sayyidi, you are my light. Thank you very much for accepting me as a mureed. I have made many mistakes towards you and have made you sad. I'm simply dust, but you always look at me, and cheer me up again when I fall. Thank you, thank you very much for all this time you have guided me, my parents and my family.

I was in my late 20's and early 30's when I consistently felt uneasiness in my heart. I did not realize I was searching or seeking a shaykh or a Tariqah or spirituality. In fact, in all my Islamic education, I had not been exposed to Tasawwuf. All I knew was that I did not feel easy in my heart, and I was not feeling peace in my ibadah. I wanted to find a way to feel at peace in my heart.

I had been informed of Shaykh Hisham's public talks when he came to Singapore, and I started attending since 2009. I always enjoyed Mawlana's talks and found comfort in them. Back then I had not started attending the private events for the mureeds. Once I was invited to a private event with Shaykh Hisham. I had driven to the door of the house where Mawlana was hosted and I actually decided to turn around and drive home without entering. That was because I had been taught that shaykhs can read our hearts and I felt like my heart was dirty.

Slowly but surely, I started attending more events and started coming for weekly dhikr. I was not sure about bay`a. Mawlana had given bay`a at one event I attended, and I took it reluctantly at the time because I was not sure I wanted the extra commitments. Bottom line was that I just was not sure about Tariqah. But I started listening to suhbahs on Sufilive and I started learning and I slowly felt better in my heart. The next event I attended when Mawlana gave bay`a, I eagerly took it, this time fully and truly wanting bay`a.

The first thing that started dissipating was the sadness and depression I used to feel daily. For this I was truly grateful. I cannot profess to be an expert or that I finally mastered all the answers. I am still learning. I am still struggling. I still feel like my heart is dirty. But I am forever grateful for a teacher and master like Mawlana Shaykh Hisham. For him to travel the world to visit us, to teach us, to comfort us, to allow us to sit in his presence is a most precious gift. I look forward to each visit and wish Mawlana would stay longer each time. Now, even knowing that I carry sins, I shamelessly seek to sit in Mawlana's presence anytime he is in Singapore.

Mawlana taught me to love Prophet ﷺ and Allah Almighty and to seek to better myself, clean myself and purify my heart for Allah's sake and Allah's pleasure. Mawlana taught me the immense and indescribable value of Mawlid. Mawlana made me feel honored to be a Muslim instead of in the past when I took it for granted that I was born a Muslim. Mawlana taught me to love Islam, to seek knowledge and that knowledge is limitless. Mawlana opened my eyes and the eyes of my heart to the true beauty of Islam and the immeasurable and unending value of Rasulullah ﷺ in this world and in the next.

Shaykh Hisham is my door to Shaykh Nazim. With Shaykh Hisham's permission, I was granted the opportunity to visit Mawlana Shaykh Nazim in March 2014. Mawlana Shaykh Nazim is the most beautiful and generous and kind and special man. Shukranlillah, shukran ya Rabbi for Mawlana Shaykh Nazim and Mawlana Shaykh Hisham and for guiding us to them and granting us to be with them. I trust their teachings and I trust them. I find safety and comfort in taking them as my guides.

Ya Allah, Ya Rabbi, please grant Shaykh Hisham divine help, divine support and divine power to lead us and to guide us. Ya Allah, Ya Rabbi, please grant them every goodness and happiness here and Hereafter. Please grant us to be at their feet dunya and Akhirah. Amin.

Around October of 2010, I began feeling extreme pain from my lower back through my hip and all the way down to my right leg. It was so painful I couldn't even stand to pray. The pain kept getting worse and worse, to the point I couldn't take it and decided to go to a fellow mureed who happened to be one of the top orthopedic surgeons in Michigan. After reviewing my X-rays, he recommended that I get an MRI which would show more detail.

The MRI's showed that I had a herniated disc at L5S1, which was causing all the pain. After seeing it, they looked at me in amazement and remarked that I must have a very high-level tolerance for pain. I did have lots of pain, but it was tolerable. Immediately, I realized that my Shaykh's blessing was minimizing my pain.

Both the MRI Radiologist, who also happens to be a mureed, as well as the orthopedic surgeon assured me there is no way I will be cured except by an operation that involves inserting a screw and it would restrict my ability to carry heavy weights or sit for long journeys. He immediately recommended for me not to carry anything over 5 pounds and that I should even not fly on long trips.

I was shocked to say the least and thought, "How am I going to do my job?" which requires flying all over the world and even to the Far East at least twice a year, sometimes 20 hours of flight time with a stop in Japan! And of course I need to carry 50 pounds or more of luggage.

I informed Mawlana Shaykh Hisham, for whom I work as his assistant and cameraman. He looked at me and smiled. I felt shy to ask him for a cure as I knew if Awliya are asked they must get permission from Prophet ﷺ, and they feel shy to ask except for all that are in the same situation.

Our very next trip was to Argentina and Chile. I knew it was going to be a painful experience but with the blessings and support of my Shaykh, I went and that's when I witnessed the miracle. Never did I feel the pain on the plane, even though I was sitting for hours on end, and the pain even disappeared while praying. I could even carry heavy bags with no pain afterwards.

There are many moments I can remember where Mawlana Shaykh Hisham helped me any way he could. The day everyone was yelling at me, he said "So, they are making you tired." The day we were all exhausted, frustrated and hot, he said, "I feel like we left Jannah and went to Jahannam." But the thing I pray for most is the support to come. The support I will need for all that I want to do, and of course his support Hereafter! Happy Birthday! We love you and thank you!

When I first met you at Singapore Expo, something wonderful triggered in my heart. When Shaykh was presenting his speech, I knew he was the "One". True enough, my life has been a blessing from Allah Almighty and Mawlana's guidance. I was extremely happy when I sent in my request for bay`a through the internet and it was accepted. Our hearts connected. I never felt so happy in my life. Thank you Mawlana, may Allah Almighty bless you and your family. Happy birthday once again.

Towards the back of the upper floor of the Burton Mosque, a group of girls sit together happily. Some of them live nearby, while others have driven for hours just to stay for the weekend. Maghrib is soon, and it is almost time to eat. After the food, more dhikr, and the Tahajjud prayer, they will head back to their separate homes and temporary lodgings. Some of them stay up talking and laughing with their cousins until suhoor. The familiarity of their houses is miles away, but here with each other is another home.

Mawlana brings light into our lives, not only through his spiritual guidance and sometimes life-altering advice, but also through his hospitality, which brings people together from around the world and forms a community unlike any other. Thank you Mawlana, for bringing amazing friends into my life, and for creating a community to enjoy their company in.

There are so many wonderful and amazing things to say about Mawlana. It is hard to choose just one. So I will start near the beginning and describe an early-on experience.

I became a follower of Mawlana nearly 20 years ago. When I was first Muslim, my husband was not, but he wanted to go to the Hajj as he liked to travel and was really searching his soul for spiritual answers. He was not interested in being Muslim, but thought that he might find some truth on a pilgrimage.

One night we found ourselves at a book-signing in Berkeley. He decided to ask Mawlana how he could go to Hajj. He stood in line to speak to him. When he was next in line, Mawlana looked at him and, without asking him what he wanted, he said, "By plane." He told my husband he would have to take his hand first. My husband took his hand and repeated Mawlana's words. Then Mawlana asked him if he knew he had just become a Muslim. He said, "Yes." I was astounded! Later that night my husband said he could not remember what happened. A few years later, however, he did ask Mawlana to be his shaykh and began to follow the Sufi path.

Shaykh Hisham Kabbani inspires me with knowledge of Haqq. Without a doubt Shaykh Hisham is special. His love for the Prophet ﷺ cannot be described in words, but in his lectures you can see the real love of his Creator and the Messenger.

What can I say about Sultan al-Awliya Shaykh Hisham Kabbani? There are no words to describe our Shaykh's beauty, his love for his mureeds and the stations of sainthood that he resides on. I cannot share all the karamaat of our Holy Shaykh, but since there is permission I will share only one event.

Shaykh came to our city for a few days and old mureeds had the honor to host him. We sat for suhbah and after dhikr everyone went home after Shaykh left. On my drive back home, I was thinking to myself how lucky are the mureeds who can host our Shaykh, and I wished my home was nice enough to host Shaykh. How lucky and blessed are those homes that Shaykh's feet touch. With a heavy heart I went back home and went to sleep. Later that night at around 4:00 am I woke up, and I found myself standing on the stairs of my house and Shaykh Hisham was standing there at the door. I saw his Holy face with my own eyes then he disappeared.

This is how Shaykh looks after our desires even when we don't have means to fulfill them. How lucky am I and how blessed is my home that Shaykh Hisham's holy feet touched it. Connection to Shaykh Hisham through our heart is more important that physical contact. May Allah give Mawlana my life also, all the happiness and contentment in this life and may Allah give us all the honor to be under his feet on the Day of Judgment. Ameen thumma ameen.

I was under the impression that I was the bee seeking your nectar and then it dawned on me that I am not the bee; rather, you are the bee gathering sweet nectar from Beloved Muhammad ﷺ and from Allah Almighty making heavenly honey and I…I am the wild, untamed bear hungry for your honey. Like the bear, I must work to reach your honey. If I am patient and have courage to correct my character, I will surely find it.

Even when I can't completely see where the honey is to eat from it, I can feel it's presence; I am drawn to its heavenly sent, its sweet fragrance, and that is why I had to return. I had to be near the fragrance of your honey even if I cannot yet eat from it.

I have struggled a lot in my life, and over the last few years I have come to realize that my struggles came from not wanting to be disciplined. I was so miserable and unhappy. I am discovering that happiness and inner peace is in being disciplined, in having good manners, in being patient when difficulties come, that the difficulties polish and cleanse us and make life sweet, if we realize it.

It has happened many times that I have felt something lifted and a new perspective becomes available to me. I believe you are a part of that. You are the rock in my life, unchanging, solid, and showing me the way to a good life here and in the Hereafter.

I have searched with my heart, but no one else carries the truth that I see in you. You have something no one else does. You have a purity about you that I can't seem to find elsewhere. I am at your service. Best of wishes to you and your beautiful family.

After ladies' dhikr with Hajjah, Mawlana came into the room. He and Hajjah were throwing flowers and sweets. I was standing with my hands down by my sides, almost hidden behind a pillar and hemmed in from all directions and said to myself, "Don't push, if you are meant to get something, you will." Almost immediately a sweet flew straight into my hand—down by my side, squashed in a crowd! Then a rose, thrown by Hajjah, came so close that all I had to do was raise my hand to catch it.

In another story, I went to Umrah. I took the small red Naqshbandi Handbook that Mawlana produced. I read only the du`as from this book—everything opened up through that book. I was able to get into the Rawda Shareef every time I went, many sisters in our group only managed one visit. SubhaanAllah.

Once I was late in arriving at the Haram in Mecca, so I couldn't get inside for the jama`at prayers. The guard wouldn't let me through the barrier, but I could see the Ka'aba and was reading different du`a from the Handbook. On reading the Du`a of Rajab practices that says something like, "I am entering through the door of sinners and whoever comes to Your Door, do not turn them away," subhanAllah, the guard suddenly said something, I looked up, his face was shining with light and he opened the barrier and let me in.

Alhamdulillah wa shukranlillah, I have been blessed to follow and be guided by one of the greatest Awliya of our time who has dedicated his life to Islam and tirelessly worked for the nation of Muhammad ﷺ. This is none other than our beloved Sayyidi Mawlana Shaykh Muhammad Hisham Kabbani.

Shaykh Hisham has been one of the major figures in my life, always guiding me and supporting me through hard times. Though I have never been in his company physically, I always feel him close to me spiritually and from time to time appearing in my dreams. A few years ago, I lost my way and turned away from Islam completely as if I was Muslim just by name. There was no one that could have pulled me from the dark pit I was stuck in. Alhamdulillah, the spiritual pull of Mawlana was so strong I made an intention to change one day and soon found Sufilive. If it was not for Shaykh Hisham, for sure 100% I would have ended up on the streets drowning in sins.

May Allah Subhanahu wa Ta'ala bless Shaykh Hisham and grant him a long, healthy life to reach the time of Sayyidna Mahdi (as) and Sayyidna Isa (as). May Allah Subhanahu wa Ta'ala grant him more and more and elevate his stations in the Presence of Prophet Muhammad ﷺ.

As a child, I remember going to Upstate New York and Mawlana Shaykh Nazim, Shaykh Hisham and his family were there. They were getting ready for a barbecue. Shaykh Hisham was barbecuing lamb amidst the smoke and heat. I got to have some of the lamb and alhamdulillah it was the best tasting lamb that I have ever had, even today thirty years later.

Mawlana Shaykh Hisham has taught and still teaches us endlessly. From every moment there is a something to be learned, if we can only stop and hear. We are so in need. Thank you for your endless help, guidance and love! Shukran ya Rabbi for sending us such a one to help us in this dunya, Akhirah and towards Your Beloved Sayyidina Muhammad ﷺ.

I have seen indisputable signs that Mawlana Shaykh Hisham has been with me throughout my life, not just from the day we met. He also blesses and protects my entire family, which includes non-Muslims who see his miracles and love him. After I met Shaykh Hisham, one day my mom was very upset about her granddaughter, who was in big problems. I said to her, "Mom, I think you know what you have to do." She looked at me and, without prompting, raised her right index finger and we read the Shahadah! How did she know to do that? When I later saw Mawlana, he humbly said, "Congratulations on your mother taking Shahadah. She did that because of you." Over the years I had asked my mom dozens of times and she never accepted. We know all good things that come to us are from Mawlana's baraka. May everything we hold dear be his ransom on Qiyamah.

Dear Mawlana,

I had always wondered why people would act all weird when they meet a celebrity, but when I came to visit you, I finally understood.

Mawlana, you are so sweet, kind, humble, nice, soft hearted, funny, gentle, caring, oh words cannot describe how good you are.

Mawlana, I really love you, you have changed my life completely, and I am so thankful for that.

You are always there for me, praying for me and my family, and protecting me. I can't ever thank you for all this.

May Allah make you and your whole family much more happiness and give you and your family a happy, healthy long life.

Happy Birthday!

Wishing our beloved Mawlana a blessed birthday and may Allah Almighty grant him many more. Ameen. We only wish to express our love and gratitude to Mawlana. We all love you, Sayyidi, and are thankful to Allah Almighty for guiding us towards you.

He gives us the gift of knowing ourselves, finding ourselves under his watchful and loving gaze, masha'Allah. He guides us to ourselves and in the process of doing so, we are given the honored and esteemed opportunity to get to know him better, through which we get to know our Beloved Prophet ﷺ better and ultimately have knowledge of our Lord Insha'Allah, as per the hadith that, "Who knows himself, knows his Lord," each according to their own level and capacity of understanding.

Building a relationship with Sayyidi Shaykh Hisham is akin to building one's relationship with Allah Almighty, as he is the true vicegerent of his Lord. The difficulties and troubles of our lives and in the world that he makes right give us a taste and glimpse of Al-Adil's Justice. As he stands up for all that is true in religion and life in general, we experience Al-Haqq's truth upheld by His Truthful Warrior, Madad al-Haqq.

When he treats our spiritual illnesses in the way only a true master can, with his brilliant mind, we feel the tremendous wisdom of Al-Hakim. The mercy he shows us when we have wronged ourselves and he supplicates on our behalf, and we instantaneously feel better, helps us understand Allah's Beautiful Names Ar-Rahman and Ar-Rahim. His tender care and concern for each and every soul he comes across, illustrates the Love of Al-Wadud. No other person on the face of the Earth can compare in importance to him, the one who guides us to our destiny according to the ayah, "For every one there is a direction."

He is of an exalted character, walking in the footsteps of our Beloved Prophet ﷺ. Illuminating the way for mankind to take hold of his holy jubba that we may join him and share in his heavenly ascension and ibadah. He is our salvation, the personification of the Holy Qur'an and Hadith, bringing the holiness of their words to life. As no one can possibly know the greatness of Prophet ﷺ except Allah Azza wa Jal, none can truly know the greatness of our beloved murshid, Mawlana Shaykh Hisham Kabbani except Prophet ﷺ and Allah Almighty. For he is a hidden treasure, as is his Lord.

Dear Mawlana Shaykh Hisham, Happy Birthday and thank you for all that you do for us! I met you recently for the Mawlid celebration in London. You looked at me and smiled and I kissed your hand, and that was it, but I have never felt such a feeling of serenity and love in all my life. It awakened something in me. At the dhikr which you led two days later I felt it again. The suhbah after the dhikr resonated with me immensely. Things I have been thinking about for years seemed to be answered. I pray to be in your presence again Mawlana and that Allah bless you and give you long life insha'Allah. Happy Birthday ya Sayyidi, I love you.

Once I was completing a task and I was experiencing lots of difficulties. Alhamdullillah when the task was finally completed, I received a call from Mawlana Shaykh Hisham.

"Are you happy?" Mawlana asked.

"Yes, Sayyidi," I answered. "With your baraka the task was completed. It is quite amazing; it's like you have a camera on me. I just finished the task, and you called to enquire about it."

"Even if you are in the deepest ocean, I can still see you."

"Sayyidi, you are reminding me of my dream. You came to my house and you were welcomed. You were wearing white clothes full of light, and your face was shining like a full moon as you made dhikr. When I saw you, I was astonished. Your reply was a nice smile with a tender look, full of mercy."

Then Mawlana made du`a, and the phone call was ended.

How gentle, how delicate, how subtle, how merciful, how humble Mawlana is.

He has the ability to see our actions, our deepest thoughts, what we hide and what we show. Indeed, Prophet ﷺ said, "Beware of the insight of the Believer for verily, he sees with the light of Allah ﷻ." Although he has this ability to see, he puts a veil on our shortcomings, sins and mistakes. Most of us, especially myself, with such power would become tyrannical.

May Allah Almighty help us acquire a drop of Mawlana's beautiful characters. Ameen.

Happy Birthday to you as we thank Allah Almighty for your presence on this continent and around the world, for providing us certainty in our hearts that our Prophet ﷺ is with us. No words to express our love and gratitude to you Sayyidi, but just saying shukr for your patience with us as you carry out the heavy task of changing our personalities from haivwaan to insaan (we pray that we are not letting you down) and bear witness to Allah Almighty that you truly have made a difference to everyone in these dark and confusion filled days.

Alhamdulillah wa shukrulillah. Madad, madad, madad ya Sayyidim, madad. We are asking with all our bad adab, astaghfirullah, for your nazar always.

I was a lost soul shrouded in darkness with no clear direction and objective in my life until the day I met you Ya Sayyidi, you opened my eyes and heart to so many wonderful things to which I am eternally grateful. The best present that we could give you is to practice what you communicate so clearly and eloquently to us. Ya Sayyidi, you are simply the best. Happy Birthday!

Long ago at the Seven Sisters Priory, mureeds told us lovely stories of Mawlana Shaykh Nazim's early days in UK and their impressions of Mawlana Shaykh Hisham. One day they asked, "Ya Sayyidi, we call Mawlana Shaykh 'Shaykh Baba', so what should we call you?" Mawlana Shaykh Hisham smiled wide and said, "You can call me 'Shaykh Mama'!"

Shaykh Hisham—his name brings a smile on my face. Just a thought of him lights up my heart. I love Shaykh Hisham so much. I wonder, since I'm just an ordinary person, and I feel so much love for him in my heart, how much love Shaykh Hisham has for people like me. I know that my love for him is due to his love for me.

I live in Toronto. I never met Shaykh Hisham. I tried many times, but something always happened and I couldn't make it. Shaykh Hisham didn't leave me alone. He didn't leave me crying. He came into my dream. I dreamt I was holding his hands, sitting on my knees, and he said to me, "If you couldn't come, it's okay, look, I came here for you." Since that day I felt a bit of relief in my heart.

Tears are pouring down my eyes. No matter what I write, it would never be enough for him. I love my Shaykh Hisham, please keep me in your prayers. Insha'Allah, one day I will be able to meet you, with your du`as. Ameen.

The first time that I came to Michigan to meet Mawlana, a woman meticulously dressed in beautiful white clothes with a sparkling white scarf wrapped around her white hair intercepted me in the hallway of the dargah. She asked me if I would like to take bay`a and I said, "Yes, I would!" As I followed her up the stairs to the mosque I thought, "Hmm, I wonder what bay`a is." In that brief moment, between the bottom and top of the staircase, I knew that wherever this group of souls was going I wanted to get on their ship and go there too. And so I took your hand, not understanding too much, but absolutely certain that I wanted to be with you.

Here I am today understanding even less, unspeakably grateful and happier than ever to be here. Before I came here I met a number of kind and accomplished people offering spiritual guidance. Like a traveler lost in a terrible storm without strength left to carry herself another step I longed to collapse at their threshold and find safety. Each time my heart said with alarm, "No! You cannot trust this one with your soul." So I dragged on until I arrived here. I looked at you, knowing that Mawlana Shaykh Nazim was next to you and I asked my heart, "Can I trust these men with my burden?" And I knew in an instant that at last I had found safety and respite. I had found guidance more divine than I ever imagined possible. I hope to rest forever!

It's really hard to express something as profound as my relationship with Mawlana, or what he means to me. He is everything. He has guided me through every stage of my life—from marriage, to pregnancies, surgeries, and the passing of my mom. Whenever there was uncertainty, there was only one to whom I could turn. And he has always guided me to the best way. How, I often wonder, do people survive without him?

After I met my husband, I wanted to give up my studies. What was the use of becoming a professional when I wanted to have kids and raise a family? "No Way!" said Mawlana. And he advised me to go to a top university that had a rigorous training program, instead of the program I wanted. I couldn't understand it at the time. It was torture. It was only many years later that things became clear. Coming from a prestigious program, I was able to take time off to have kids and be with them when they were young. When I was ready to go back to work, I was able to get a good job. No one would have taken me seriously if I'd taken time off and gone to a no-name program.

It's a small story, but a good example of how Mawlana guides us, even if we may not understand it at the time. Thank you Mawlana for everything you do for my family, the Ummah, and me. We love you and wish you the happiest of birthdays! May Allah give you and your family health, happiness and prosperity here and Hereafter!

Ya Sayyidi. What is there to say? To thank you or tell you about how much we love you, what you mean to us, or how we feel about you. You've been my father, my teacher, and my dear friend for my whole life. One of my first memories is of just you and I as a child. I remember you walking, holding your 2-year old Sajeda and you pointed out the tiniest crumb of bread that had fallen on your path, which you told me to eat.

You gave me my perfect companion in my dear wife, gave us the perfect example on how to treat each other, and offered us the perfect advice when you married us. I remember sitting on your couch at our wedding and being so in love with you, Sayyidi. My heart has never felt the same since watching you read the azaan in my baby's ear the day after his birth and calling his name up to the heavens.

I won't go into the infinite and unending impact you've had on every detail of my life or all of the wonderful miracles you've granted me to witness through your grace. But the most cherished memory that forever remains the most important of my life was when you came to me as a bird and whispered to my soul La Ilaha Il Allah.

Ya Mawlana, I do not even know where to begin. I would not be the person I am today without your guidance, you are my biggest blessing and I thank Allah Almighty every day for putting me under your wing. You have taught me to be spiritual and to love every single aspect of my religion. You have a beautiful way of relating to all people, young and old. When I was younger I had a dream that when things on earth got scary and bad, your turban became the safety belt for all of us. As long as we held on we would be okay. Mawlana, you are my safety belt! May Allah Almighty grant you many more birthdays. I love you.

One look at the faces of people surrounding Mawlana Shaykh Hisham, to see the joy and contentment in their expressions, to see the adab they have learned from him always fills me with tranquility when I am in his presence.

Mawlana walks the walk rather than just talks the talk. What better way to learn how to respect women then to see him stand up and get a chair for his wife himself when she entered his office and all the chairs were occupied.

Rather than focusing on the negative, he constantly imparts a message of universal love and fellowship. One word from Mawlana transforms people. I was 40 years old when Allah Almighty with his grace made me meet Mawlana Shaykh Hisham. Until then I would say my prayers five times a day in Ramadan and then they would soon dwindle to only Fajr every day. When I started the Naqshbandi awrad, Mawlana just told me once to remember that namaz is first and comes before the daily Naqshbandi awrad. Ten years have elapsed since then, and I have been lucky to perform all my five daily prayers. Mawlana teaches a message of moderation. I remember a dinner after Maghrib several years ago when there were two men in their early 20s at his table. They mentioned to him that they wanted to study Islam in detail and he was telling them about different types of advanced Islamic studies available in different countries. One of them then said that his parents do not want him to spend his time on Islamic studies but to work for this world. In response, Mawlana narrated a saying of Hazrat Ali Ra that people should keep one foot in this world and one in the Hereafter. I pray that Allah Almighty grant Mawlana Shaykh Hisham and his family good health and bless us with his company for many more decades.

May Allah give you every happiness for giving up your life for us, for making our lives easier, for carrying us, for loving us. We love you and hope to be with you here and Hereafter.

Mawlana Shaykh Hisham, is like a never ending ocean of love. He can take you out of the greatest depths of darkness and fill every corner of it with light. I can't imagine what my life would be like if it wasn't for my beloved teacher Shaykh Hisham. Any moment of sadness disappears just by remembering him. Every difficulty I have faced, by his baraka and du`as, becomes easy and small. There is no one alive today like him, who has touched more hearts and saved more people. The positive impact he has on everyone, even those who have only seen him once, is phenomenal. Many of my non-Muslim friends are always astonished when they see him and even years later hold him in high respect.

We were told to share experiences and miracles but the fact is Shaykh Hisham is a miracle. Nowhere else have I ever seen so many people, with so many different backgrounds, races, colors, etc., come together as one with love to one another. This is due to the teachings of Shaykh Hisham and the bridges he has built and his emphasis on unity. In these days of confusions, Sayyidi is the opener of truth and the one who has revived the Love of Prophet ﷺ across the globe.

"You will be resurrected with those whom you love" I love Shaykh Hisham. Insha'Allah May Allah Almighty grant him a longer, healthy, happy, blessed life and the same for his family. Insha'Allah may we celebrate his birthday in the time of Sayyidna Mahdi and Sayyidna Isa ﷺ. Happy Birthday! We love you!

I pray to become a better student of Mawlana Shaykh Hisham. Because of my human defects I sometimes find myself feeling unworthy of being so blessed as to have him in my life. May Allah and His Prophet Muhammad ﷺ continue to bless and raise Mawlana Shaykh Hisham, and may He bless us all to realize more Shaykh Hisham's significance. May we, no matter our state or position, become the Ummah he is guiding us to be. May Allah and His Prophet Muhammad ﷺ bless me and grant us all to abide in the Grace of The One Heart. For our benefit, may Allah bless Mawlana Shaykh Hisham with many birthdays to come in this earthly realm. Amin.

Alhamdulillah, we are very fortunate to have the presence of a Wali among us. May Allah give our Shaykh good health and long life, ameen. I was going through a tough time in life, when a good friend of mine introduced me to Sufism and I started to go to the gathering with him. When I met Mawlana for the first time I felt that he was not an ordinary person. He made me feel at home, welcome, and very special. After I left Michigan I was not the same person anymore. I felt very spiritual and detached from material things. I didn't want to live in Los Angeles any longer, and finally I spoke to Mawlana and I decided to move to Michigan and live close to Shaykh.

I started working at the farm and also lived there. After a few months living at the farm, I realized it is like a rehab. The purpose of living there is to get rid of bad characteristics. There were rules and regulations that weren't easy for me, but Mawlana was very patient and loving. He taught me how to forgive people and to not keep anger or hate in my heart.

After a few months of living at the farm, one day I went to talk to Mawlana and Hajjah. I said, "It has been a few years I am praying to Allah to forgive my sins." Mawlana made a du`a for me that Allah except my du`a and Hajjah taught me a very special du`a that I should read every day.

After a couple of months, I had a dream that Mawlana Shaykh Nazim was saying, "Grandshaykh and Prophet Mohammad ﷺ went to Allah Almighty and they asked for forgiveness on your behalf." Then Mawlana Shaykh Nazim said, "Allah forgives you." This was a huge step for me in Tariqah.

A few weeks later, I grew very sick and my whole body was collapsing. I had high fever and all my body wasn't moving. At this time, I knew for sure this is not just a sickness and I passed out. When I opened my eyes in the morning, I saw from a small window on the roof. Someone was leaving. Mawlana Shaykh Hisham was all night watching me, making du`a for my life.

Oh Mawlana, Mawlana! How can I thank you for what you have done for me? You stay all night awake to protect me or save my life. You use your power to fight Shaytan for us or you make du`a to extend our life and you never give up on us.

One very important teaching he has is love—love Allah, love Prophet ﷺ, love Awliya Allah and love people. Insha'Allah I will reach there one day soon. Ameen. May Allah Almighty raise his maqam to Jannat al-Firdous and give him long and healthy life. Ameen.

Recently, I was invited to go overseas to perform Mawlid and Qasidah. It was a long journey, and I would be away from my wife on the other side of the world for about 12 days. My previous trips to perform had been rather closer to home and no more than a week. My wife felt alone each time I went, and I also felt she needs the extra care from me even when far away.

There was uncertainty as to whether I should go, since my wife would be left alone, again. I usually liked to take her with me wherever I went, but sometimes that was just not possible.

So I called Mawlana and spoke with him, asking for his advice. Immediately he said, "You go, it will be good openings for you. Your wife, don't worry, we are taking care of her."

You cannot imagine the weight, which was on my shoulder falling off instantly by those beautiful words. When I told my wife, she was in tears, yet happy to know that our Master and Teacher gave such a resounding assurance!

So I went for the trip and was back safely 2 weeks later. A week into my return, my wife recalled that during the entire time I wasn't around, she actually felt very safe, in fact, she felt safer and more secure than she had experienced with my past trips! She actually didn't feel anything at all, right until my return.

We believe that demonstrates the truth in Mawlana's words that he will take care of his mureeds and we felt it too! Truly, Mawlana's karamah and love shine in each moment of our lives!

I don't really know anything but I know I love you. From my earliest memory to now, I remember always being excited that I was going to see you. Just being in the same room, knowing your presence is there makes me happy. All my worries and problems disappear when I see you. I feel at ease and free like a spec flowing in your Oceans of Greatness. We are so lucky to have you, words cannot describe. You show us the most beautiful Islam and make everything clear. Thank you for everything you have done for me, even though there is nothing that is enough to thank you. May Allah grant you eternal happiness.

Sayyidi Mawlana Shaykh Hisham, you are one who pulled me out from darkness and filled my life with light and hope. I had asked Prophet ﷺ on His Birthday ash-Shareef to give me a gift by helping me to find the Pious and the Saaliheen, and to be with them. Then I found you. I don't have the words to describe how honored I feel to be granted to be in your Presence.

You are Khalifa of Allah Almighty in our universe. May He dress you with health, long life and heavenly power to carry the Ummah.

One day, Mawlana decided to make a soup from the leftovers in the fridge. We were in Oakland and I was helping in the kitchen that summer. He literally took all the leftovers regardless of the type – pasta, sujook, beans, leftover soup and other dishes that I cannot recall. I was very surprised, wondering what this very odd mix would taste like. At some point, Mawlana asked me to give him the leftover watermelon pieces. I made a weird face, but then he smiled and said it was a joke. He added some mango-pickle to the pot, a few spices and let the whole mixture cook. I was wondering what it would taste like, without any willingness to actually taste it. So I disappeared from the kitchen before it was ready. When the soup was done, he asked someone to call me to try it out. I couldn't say no, so I made a plate and decided to try it. Before eating, I made a du`a asking Allah to clean me from all the impurities in my body. Then I ate and that soup was the best food I had ever had in my life! It was so tasty. I was just amazed.

May Allah and His Prophet Muhammad ﷺ continue to bless and raise Mawlana Shaykh Hisham, and may He bless us all to realize more Shaykh Hisham's significance. May Allah and His Prophet Muhammad ﷺ bless me and us all to abide in the Grace of the One Heart. For our benefit, may Allah bless Mawlana Shaykh Hisham with many birthdays to come in this earthly realm. Amin.

In the many years I have been blessed to be in the company of Mawlana Shaykh Hisham Kabbani, one of the dearest, subtle truths, he has illuminated within my heart, insha'Allah, the concept of being "From you to you." Having the blessed opportunity of partaking in many of Mawlana's outreach and educational endeavors was an honor in and of itself. However, the lessons one learns and experiences in doing so are indispensable.

Over the years, in doing any little thing with the intention of it being "for Mawlana," it slowly became very apparent that the greatest benefactor of such intentions was me, astaghfirullah; hence, anything done "from me" turned out to be essentially "for me," in Allah's Generosity, mirrored by His Prophet ﷺ and Awliyaullah. Mawlana Shaykh Hisham has given me many specific du`as or ayahs of the Qur'an to read in the past for different reasons, be it marriage, health, ease in difficulty, etc. These are cherished words, so at some point in reflection, it dawned on me that I should read what Mawlana taught me for him and his family, a manifest variation of, "From him to him!"

As he raised me with certain manners and love from the heart, we used what he taught us to honor him, masha'Allah. This is again, from you to you. In all of this, nothing stands out more prominently than the fact that all is One. La ilaha illa-Llah Muhammad ar-Rasulullah.

One look at the faces of people surrounding Mawlana Shaykh Hisham, to see the joy and contentment in their expressions, to see the adab they have learned from him, always fills me with tranquility when I am in his presence.

Mawlana walks the walk rather than just talks the talk. What better way to learn how to respect women then to see him stand up and get a chair for his wife himself when she entered his office and all the chairs were occupied.

Rather than focusing on the negative, he constantly imparts a message of universal love and fellowship. One word from Mawlana transforms people. Mawlana teaches a message of moderation. I once heard him narrate a saying from Sayyidna Ali, "People should keep one foot in this world and one in the Hereafter."

I pray that Allah Almighty grants Mawlana Shaykh Hisham and his family good health and bless us with his company for many more decades.

May Allah give you every happiness for giving up your life for us, for making our lives easier, for carrying us, for loving us. We love you and hope to be with you here and Hereafter.

Happy Birthday, Mawlana! Thank you for everything. Being with you is like being in Madinat an-Nabi ﷺ.

Looking at them I am reminded of our Beloved Mawlana Shaykh Nazim. I just want to send my love in and that I think they truly are amazing. I wish I could follow them around the world and be in their noble company always.

I have never personally met Shaykh Hisham; however, in a way I feel like I personally know him. I was introduced to the Naqshbandi Tariqah and few years ago and have been fascinated by its teachings thanks to Shaykh Nazim, may he rest in peace, and Shaykh Hisham. I would also like to wish Shaykh Hisham a very Happy Birthday.

Dear Mawlana, from the bottom of my heart, I want to wish you a happy birthday. You always make us joyful, peaceful and thankful for all that Allah Almighty provided us: love. Love of the Most Beloved One, love of our dearest Shuyukh, love among mureeds and family.

One night, I dreamt that I was back in my home country and there was a lot of turmoil. I remember something heavy like a war or earthquake was about to take place. There was so much panic; people were running all around and suddenly we saw from down a hill a tremendous amount of dust that was coming in our direction. We were all shaking.

As that dust approached, we saw in fact that it was a horseman on a white horse, wearing all white except for his green turban. He had a long white beard. He was galloping and saying some words which I believe were 'Allahu Akbar.' After his passage, I noticed a group of people wearing black sleeves, so calm in this panicky environment that I followed them. They went to a secret place where they were doing dhikr.

A few days later, I took bay`a during Mawlid an-Nabi ﷺ, because my heart was so demanding of love that night. A few months later, I came to meet you for the first time in Fenton at the farm, where I recognized that beautiful and powerful horseman from my dream. You guided me towards this path of love. For that Mawlana, I will be always thankful. I wish the most blessed and beloved birthday to you, dear Guide.

We are grateful to Allah Subhanahu wa Ta'ala that in His Ultimate Wisdom He created us in this time and guided us to the best of those upon whom He has favored and drawn near as His friend.

Oh our beloved Murshid, you are the reed flute through which the breath of wisdom flows, calling others to join in sincere yearning for The One and praise for His Beloved Prophet ﷺ. Wherever you go, voices raise up in remembrance of their Lord and praise for His Beloved Prophet ﷺ. You are our conductor, our inspiration and proof that despite our being out of tune, through love and sincerity you will carry us and present us in the best way.

We ask that Allah Almighty bless you and grant you long life, that He keep us in your company all the days of our lives and that He bestow upon you the best of rewards. In gratitude to Allah Almighty and with deep affection for you, we wrap up our joy and present it with this salutation: Allahumma salli alaa Sayyidina Muhammad wa alaa aali Sayyidina Muhammad and Happy Birthday, Sayyidi Shaykh Muhammad Hisham Kabbani!

My parents told me once that when I was around the age 2-3 years, I could only say short and simple words. Remarkably, once at that age, I was looking at a picture of you and then said to my mom, "Mama, I really love Mawlana."

Then when I was fifteen, my family and I moved to a bigger city. I was naive, and I tended to put myself in precarious positions. The crowds and the energy of the city were too much on my nerves; I started to develop severe stomach pains and nausea. It became so hard to keep food down that I stopped eating altogether.

My mother wasn't sure what to do with me. She invited Mawlana and Hajjah to our house. My mom brought me into the room where Mawlana was staying. I stood there with my hair dangling in my face. He asked me to sit down. I shuffled over to the chair and schlepped down into it. Then he asked someone to bring some food. I told him that I couldn't eat, but disregarding my protests, he told the man to bring the food. He placed the plate in front of me. I looked down at it, it was lahmajun. I looked up at Mawlana and said that I couldn't eat this. He just kept insisting I eat. I was not looking forward to throwing up again, but I complied.

When I started eating, there was no nausea. I ate and ate, I couldn't stop eating, and he just kept bringing them. I must have eaten ten. Mawlana was laughing.

Sayyidi Mawlana Shaykh Hisham, you are the one who pulled me out from darkness and filled my life with light and hope. I had asked Prophet ﷺ on His Birthday to give me a gift by helping me to find the Pious and the Saaliheen, and to be with them. Then I found you. I don't have the words to describe how honored I feel to be granted to be in your Presence.

You are a Khalifa of Allah Almighty in our universe. May Allah Almighty dress you with health and long life and heavenly power to carry the Ummah.

Allah Almighty sent us a Wali to help us in a time of need, and we thank Allah every day for giving us a chance to see him and listen to him. Happy Birthday, Mawlana and may Allah Almighty give you good health and long life.

On your birthday, I pray to Allah Almighty that He grant you the best of dunya and Akhirah. May He, in His Infinite Mercy, elevate your darajaat and shower His Blessings upon you and your family. I have never had the pleasure of meeting you, but I possessed a black tasbeeh that you had given out to mureeds during Hajj in Madina. It was my most prized possession, but somehow it disappeared over time and it saddens me deeply. I hope and pray that we can meet soon.

For me, Shaykh Hisham is the way of life. Since knowing him, my life has become happier and more peaceful. Happy Birthday my beloved Shaykh Hisham Kabbani. May Allah Almighty bless you with long life, and good health.

Ya Mawlana, I do not even know where to begin. I would not be the person I am today without your guidance. You are my biggest blessing and I thank Allah Subhanahu wa Ta'ala every day for putting me under your wing. You have taught me to be spiritual and to love every single aspect of my religion. You have a beautiful way of relating to all people, young and old. When I was younger, I had a dream that when things on earth got scary and bad, your turban became the safety belt for all of us and that as long as we held on we would be okay. Mawlana, you are my safety belt! May Allah Subhanahu wa Ta'ala grant you many more years. I love you.

I'm eternally grateful for the birth of Mawlana Shaykh Hisham. One gaze from Mawlana is a life-changing experience. It makes me feel like a butterfly. Alhamdullilah wa shukrulillah.

We love you more than the word 'love' itself. May Allah Almighty bless you endlessly and raise you higher and grant you the longest of lives Insha'Allah. Happy Birthday, Mawlana! We love you!

Dear Respected Mawlana, As-salamu alaykum wa rahmatullahi wa barakatahu.

Alhamdulillah, following in your footsteps, I've taken up residence in Jeddah. It is truly a humbling experience to be close to the Holy Sanctuaries and I am trying my best to make the most of this unique opportunity Allah has blessed me with. I often wish that we can meet soon in person! So many questions I'd like your help with. Chief among these is how I can progress further on this great, blessed path. Since you prescribed those simple yet powerful awrad for me I have seen tangible improvements in all aspects of my being, alhamdulillah! Of course, I realize there are other ways we keep in touch by the grace of Allah, so I await your guidance with great anticipation. Your weak disciple.

Poems

O Mawlana, we were lost, and you found us. We were wandering, and you took us in.

We were hungry, and you fed us. We were thirsty, and you slaked our thirst. We were dirty, and you cleansed us.

O Mawlana, we were frightened, and you comforted us. We were crying, and you dried our tears. We were weak, and you strengthened us. We were weary, and you gave us the energy to go on.

O Mawlana, we were choking on the offal of this existence, and you nourished us with the fruit of knowledge.

O Mawlana, we were nauseated by the stench of our sins, and you filled our nostrils with the perfume of Jannah.

O Mawlana, our ears were ringing with the noise of this world, and you silenced it with the sound of dhikr.

O Mawlana, our eyes were burning from the things we had seen, and you quenched them with the Light of Muhammad ﷺ.

How can we ever thank you? How can we ever repay these debts? How can we give you anything when you are rich in Allah's baraka and we are such poor disciples?

We have nothing but our love for you. All we have is our longing to be at your feet. For we know that you sit at the feet of him who sits at the feet of the Almighty. Through you, we are connected to the one who traveled to the highest heaven, and through him we are connected to the One.

I am writing
to ask you
be gentle with me
for I am fragile.
I wish to be soft and malleable
like wet clay.
But actually, I am a piece of cracked china
precariously perched on the edge of a table.

I pray
you will be easy on me
for I am weak.
I wish to be spring's bud
ready to bloom
into summer's beauty.
Instead, I am
a pile of dry autumn leaves
brittle under your feet.

Of course you know all this
(and more).

Still I ask you
mold me softly,
grow me gently,
and always keep me company.

You are my star on a dark night
You are the beacon guiding to the light
Through my masters I have achieved sight
May Allah Almighty make you shine so bright

I was somewhere new,
Felt uneasy
Then I saw something familiar
A bright blue light
And a rush of joy filled inside me
Oh it's you it's you!
For sure I was in security

Oh true one,
a wonder of
complete reflection of Sayyidna Muhammadun Rasulullah ﷺ
What miracle,
what proof
you have sent
to my heart,
to my eyes,
to my mind
more than
the ultimate reality,
the secret of existence,
the mercy
the realization of thy beauty.
sinking and drowning in this ocean of love, lifts me away from the untrue moment of existence in the body and devolves me in thy beauty,
the beauty of Muhammadun Rasulullah ﷺ.
thank you oh precious gift from our creator,
hope that Shaykh Muhammad Hisham Kabbani
the dissolver of pain
the crusher of egos
the light of darkness
the guide to happiness
the merciful for all creation
the bearer of unconditional eternal love and mercy's, spirit fills the earth.

How can you speak of the one that means everything to you?!
Without Mawlana, I would not feel life,
I would not know love,
I would not be found.
Without Mawlana, there is no happiness or joy,
Without Mawlana, I would not know the way,
Without Mawlana, my enemies would succeed,
Without Mawlana, my end would not be secure,
I am with Mawlana and that means everything to me!
He gave me safety,
He gave me real life,
He turned my darkness into light.
He showed me truth,
He dug out my heart,
He connected me,
He put me on the path,
Saved me from my existence,
Pulled me up when I fell.
Every day, every moment, I call to him and he answers.
He is there,
He is my pole,
He is the shoulder to lean on.
The one that knows exactly what I need to succeed.
Let me never be separated,
Bring me closer,
Count me amongst your loved ones.
O my King, my Majesty!
May Almighty Allah's ever-present immense mercy be upon you and your radiant Queen and all the royal family.

A shaykh is coming to do my sister's nikah; that's all I knew.
Never heard of him, never seen.
He entered the room, majestic and pure, the rest I cannot explain.
But from then on it was very simple and plain.
I had to seek and find out more.
Without a word, they urged me to explore.
And that took me to Mawlana Shaykh Nazim's door.
Awliya of Allah, they leave you admiring their sacrifices and devotion.
Whilst we're in the rat race, stuck in the commotion.
But with one thought of my shaykh, the stresses are eased.
With their voice leading zikr, the heart is more than pleased.
With every glance at my Shaykh, I know he is my door.
Which will lead me to what my soul has always been searching for.

A messenger of light in the darkness
A radiating sun giving life to all creatures
Possessor of divine secrets
A bottomless well whose depths can never be reached
A cup of water drawn from his well is enough to contain the entire spinning universe
One whose water is sweeter than honey and purer than milk
His form is a flawless diamond through which Heavenly light may be transmitted
He is the one who is from The One, who is from The One
Hu is from the One
Sultan of secrets, Sultan of light, Sultan of this time
An Endless source of Love.

Truly, our only shelter is your love.
We're not foals — still, when will we learn to stand?
At this point, I would rather be a dove.
At the pearl's core sits a grain of sand.
How can we thank you in just fourteen lines?
All of English is not roomy enough!
The old masters could cut gems from the mines;
but all we have is this handful of rough.
Who'll tell us why Bilqis sought forgiveness
when she mistook the bright floor for a pool?
It must be one whose manners are the best,
since Knowledge won't make its home with a fool.
O our Shaykh, who seeks no fame or profit —
thank you for bringing us Love for Prophet ﷺ.

When I start on the path He is my guide
When I look for love He is my enchanter.
When I fight a war He is my dagger
When I seek peace He is my ambassador.
At the feast He is my wine and my sweets
In the garden He is the scent of jasmine.

In the mine He is the ruby
In the sea He is the pearl.
In the desert He is the oasis
In the heavenly spheres He is a star.

When I seek patience He is my ultimate Master
When I burn in grief He is the censer.
When I write He is my pen and paper.
When I chase after a rhyme He is my inspiration.
When I wake up He is my awareness
When I go to sleep He haunts my dreams.
His perfection is beyond grasp, no pen or brush
Could ever describe Him.
Throw your learning let Him become your book.

There was a time in the past
When love was mentioned last
In the gatherings of learning the deen
Love of Muhammad ﷺ was seldom seen

There were dark clouds of Wahhabi monopoly
And sinister atmospheres of Salafi hegemony
Anyone who mentioned honor and Mawlid of Prophet of Harmony
Was immediately booted out of the company

Then you appeared with Mercy from Lord
To regain that lost true mantle
From the fakers and hypocrites and naysayers
To proclaim the Haqq of love and love of Haqq
To honor the love and love the honor of Muhammad ﷺ
And that Love of Muhammad ﷺ was indeed the only candle

That could disperse the darkness of ignorance
And taught that repulsive fumes of stubborn arrogance
Could only be removed by igniting the fragrance
Of Sincere Love of Muhammad ﷺ the Eminence

You came to reassure us that lovers are on Haqq
And removed all doubts and shirk
And beautified our good actions tree of obeying Muhammad ﷺ
By placing on top of it the diamond star of Love for Muhammad ﷺ

You spread Love by giving your Love
You spread Mercy by showering your mercy
You spread knowledge by sharing your knowledge
You spread tolerance by demonstrating your tolerance

Thanks to Allah for sending to us Most Honored Prophet, Sayyidul Anaam ﷺ
Thanks to Prophet Muhammad ﷺ for sending to us His Love Emissary, Shaykh Hisham
Thanks to Mawlana for teaching us about Love of Sayyidul Hisham
Thanks to All Mashaikh for demonstrating the true path of Love in Islam

Happy Birthday, Mawlana Shaykh Hisham Kabbani!
May Allah give you life of a thousand years and bless us with your du`as and company.

Your birthday a reason for celebration
A blessing beyond comprehension for this Nation.
Our Prophet ﷺ said, "Sun of Islam Will Rise From The West In The Latter Days"
This is you Sayyidi, and alhamdulillah we are trying to follow your ways.
To our Prophet and our Lord you are our door
A trustworthy hand, what could we ask for more.
Enter the palace of the Prophet through its gate
Who are you Sayyidi? a way which is straight.
The honor our Lord has given us with you as our guide
You are the reason for our pride.
Proud not of ourselves or our worthless merits
But proud to have such a Lion behind us and the one from whom he inherits.
We ask what gift we can give you our perfect master,
Without you our life would be a disaster.
We are under your Gaze, your guidance your protection,
A true master with a character dressed to perfection.
We take so much from you and give little in return,
But we have no one else to whom we can turn.
Without you no chance at all to succeed,
You are the breath of life we all need.
Please never leave us in the hands of our ego,
Or this world with its value less than the wing of a mosquito.
Please keep us with you wherever you go,
This world the next and places we do not even know.
We pray for a long healthy and wealthy life,
For you, your offspring and your beloved wife.
Our Hajjah, more valuable than our own mothers,
Fathers, children, sisters and brothers.
Blessed be your birthday and many more, Oh one with perfect behavior,
We hope to celebrate more in the time of The Savior.

Dust wanted to be known by name
Thought it will be something
In reality however it wants
It can only be dust.

Then it wanted to be known as beggar
Thought it's easier
However it tried
It can be nothing but useless.

Then it yearned to be a seeker
However it turned into jewel
With the love of Beloved ﷺ
With the touch of Shaykh.

The beggar become a seeker
In this harsh time
With the love of Awliya Allah
Otherwise who even knew
That being lover is so hard.

What words can describe the Heaven
in your pure heart
in your healing gaze
in your every breath
in your niyyat and `amal

We sought redemption and you appeared
always loving gentle forgiving
always illuminating connected
always humbly showing the way
always taking us with you

How you nurture the habitual sinners
to heal the deepest wounded hearts
to replace objections with obedience
to transform bankrupt to beloved
to give and give and give again

We exist in your magnificent Light
your acceptance is our guarantee
your smile our purification
your love our shield
your sacrifice our honor

The mirror of Sayyidina Muhammad ﷺ
oh inheritor of the Beloved
oh keeper of all the masters' secrets
oh forgiver of endless failings
oh guardian of repenting offenders

Knowing ours is an unpayable debt, we pray
may the Lord Almighty raise you in His Nearness
may His Beloved keep you forever in his noble heart
may the Sultans hold you for eternity and
may we be counted with you here and Hereafter

The darkness of my heart I didn't understand,
The darkness in my life I didn't understand.
The meaning of love I didn't know,
The complexity and ease of life I didn't know.
Your light made the dead winter inside me turn into spring,
Your nur made me see inside my own soul.
The coolness of your presence brings ease to those around you,
Your magnetism brings hope to people like me who don't deserve you,
You accepted me despite me. I could only thank you.
You understand me, the real me, like no one has understood before,
You see me, really see me, as if I have never seen myself before.
My hope, one day, perhaps I can see you too!
Love of Allah and Prophet ﷺ I thought lived inside me,
You showed me what it truly means to love The Beloved ﷺ.
Respect of Allah and Prophet ﷺ, I thought lived inside me,
You showed me how to respect, truly respect The Beloved.
My beloved Shaykh, may Allah give you a long and healthy life.
My beloved Shaykh, thank you for being an enormous blessing in my life.
My beloved Shaykh, I did not know these words as I was writing them.
My beloved Shaykh, you knew these words even before reading them.
Happy Birthday.

I sit in the presence of a great emerald tree
And delve in the depths of a vast diamond sea
Sipping the dregs of love as heavenly tea
Hoping upon hope that you will never leave
And I smile
I smile simply to be
A mere pigeon taking small gifts at your feet
And even if all you gave was your smile, so sweet
It would be enough to drown out my very heartbeat
When you smile, my worries and troubles make haste
And I smile, forgetting my pain and heartache
You smile, and at once you heal all of my burns
And I taste the Divine Peacefulness I have yearned
And we sit
We sit, and you speak of the One Lord above and
Teach us the way of submission and true love
You have delivered us from fear by casting it away
And you teach us to fear so we do not go astray
You wipe our tears and restore us to whole
And urge us to weep for the Beloved ﷺ with our souls
There are those who claim hope has forsaken us cold
But I see it shining at the foot of your threshold
Birds in the gardens only sing when you're here
Blossoms dare not bloom until you appear
And the winter erupts into spring when you're near
I shall be lost if you ever disappear
But in truth, I am lesser than the smallest grains of sand
And the knowledge is too great for me to understand
But I do not care
I don't care if I shall not ever learn the secrets my mind has failed to discern
I care not if I can fathom no secrets indeed
Because I love you, and you are all that I need.

I ask permission to pick up this pen for you,
You, who brought me up from an abyss darker than an ink pot.
And rewrote my trajectory.
You are my pen, my unwritten pages, ink from the oceans of Grace.
You are my grace, the contagious, beaming smile on my face.
You are my sun, and every star in the sky,
Lighting and mapping the way;
My overflowing vessel,
My sailing ship, my captain, the favorable wind.

You are my mirror, perfectly polished so I can see my ugliness.
You are the legacy of Nabi ﷺ, so I can try to imitate your beautiful manners.
You are my father, grandfather,
Guardian and surgeon.
You are my antidote: the honeyed syrup and the sometimes bitter pill.
You are the red pill,
You are sweet water in the desert,
Saltwater of my tears;
You are the mighty falls crashing love onto the rock of my heart.

You are the cloak I cling to in harsh climes,
The hand I grasp in blind night.
Dreams of you taste like summer,
Displeasing you tastes like death.
You are the divine accomplice breaking me out of prison;
The sledgehammer and the carpenter
The mason and the smith.
You are my knight, my liege, my king on earth.
You are my door to goodness.

Forgive me, for you act as my servant when I should be serving you.
You are the protecting thorn, and the giver of blooms;
You are the honey and the bee, the hive and the distant blossom.
You are the blizzard that makes us stay home,
And the golden crack in the clouds,
Opening the hope to glimpse your face once again.
You are the purity of snowflakes before they touch ground.

Sayyidi, you are the one who empties us,
And the one who makes us whole.
You are our link to the Most Precious Chain;
You are the Entire Chain in a single soul.

I found you, I found you
After being lost
In a long, lonely night.
I found you
Since you came
You came and you showed
You showed yourself to me
You gave me a sight.
You showed me a glimpse
Not once, not twice
But several times
You showed me the glimpse
Of your loving light.
But I lost, I lost
I lost my way
In a dark night
But when it was done
The ugly plight
I saw you for real
And I recognized
Who used to come to me
When it was alright.
I met you, I met you
And it's the happiest of sights
And I know for sure
With all my might
That everything now
is going to be alright.

It thunders here
the skies
weep.
I saw my shaykh
in my dreams
dressed in gold
and white.
they did not know
who he was
they did not cry
like me
seated
in chairs
as he spoke
in an outdoor
theater
in a place
I do not know.

Is it your face
that adorns the garden?

Is it your fragrance
that intoxicates this garden?

Is it your spirit
that has made this brook
a river of pure water?

Hundreds have looked for you
and died searching
in this garden
where you hide behind the scenes.

But this pain is not for those
who come as lovers.

You are easy to find here.

You are in the breeze
and in this river.

Illustrations

الله

By Hadi

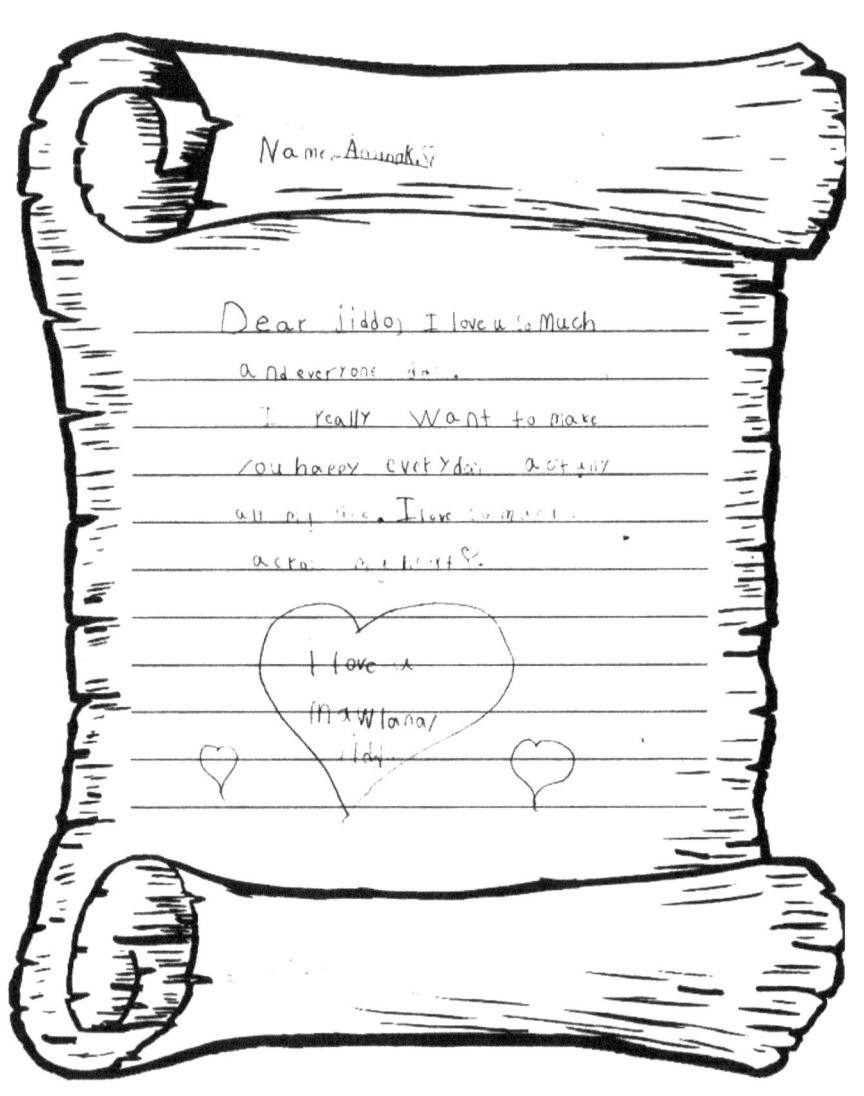

www.ingramcontent.com/pod-product-compliance
Lightning Source LLC
Chambersburg PA
CBHW041957080526
44588CB00021B/2777